Mini Pig Owners Guide:
Transitioning and Caring for Mini Pigs

By Stephanie Matlock & Kimberly Chronister

Contributors

Cathy Corrigan, DVM

Jessie Brookings
This Little Piggy Mini Pet Pigs

Stacey Davenport
Pig Pen Hill Mini Pigs

First Printing: 2016

ISBN-13: 978-1537685625

ISBN-10: 1537685627

American Mini Pig Association
PO Box 735
Aurora, Missouri, 65610

www.americanminipigassociation.com

DEDICATION

We would like to thank the ever passionate mini pig community for encouraging an environment of support and learning for all current and future mini pig owners.

American Mini Pig Association

2016

CONTENTS

Preface

The contents of this book were brought together in part by the creation of three wonderful organizations devoted to betterment of the lives of mini pigs and their owners.

This book is a basic care guide for new owners of AMPA registered piglets. We have also made this resource available to any new owner of a mini pig. This is a summary of information for new pig owners.

You can find more information related to the care and ownership of mini pigs in a full comprehensive book, Mini Pig Care, The AMPA Big Book of Mini Pigs . You can never stop learning about mini pigs, their care, health, personalities, and training. We encourage every reader to visit the American Mini Pig Association website for continued education and support.

AMPA & Nonprofits Introduction

Welcome to the American Mini Pig Association. We are making history as the first official Mini Pig Registry of its kind. The American Mini Pig Association was developed by a dedicated team of miniature pig breeders, owners, veterinarians, and rescue liaisons whom are committed to educating and advocating for miniature pigs, promoting healthy breeding practices, upholding the code of ethics for breeders and owners alike with the intent to help reduce the number of displaced pigs, bridging the gap between owners, breeders, vets, and rescues, and improving the quality of the American Mini Pig as a breed.

This association was created to become a source of factual information for everything mini pig. A collaboration of research, life experiences, veterinary medicine, and love for these animals for the public to enjoy, learn from, and share. It is a community of people joined to improve the lives of mini pigs, their owners, breeders, and rescue organizations.

We strive to educate on the joys of training. To inspire owners to turn frustrations into goals of training for a happier, healthier pig and a more fulfilling relationship with their pet. To produce not only pig owners, but advocates of good animal care and practices in their communities.

We have established two individual 501c3 non-profit organizations for education and rescue to help us accomplish our goals in the pig community. We want to inspire you to join and work with us to advocate, educate, and improve the quality of life for mini pigs and their owners.

American Mini Pig Rescue
www.AmericanMiniPigRescue.com
American Mini Pig Education
www.AmericanMiniPigEducation.com

Become a Member, Register Your Pig

Visit American Mini Pig Association.com and choose your membership level. Membership comes with a growing list of perks and privileges. You will be connected to a community of mini pig advocates and educators that work hard to build a better life for mini pigs everywhere. Current AMPA Members have been raving about the welcome packets that arrive in the mail with gifts, coupons, and educational materials. As a member you will also be eligible for members-only contests and giveaways.

Membership benefits include:

- The opportunity to register your pig and receive added benefits
- Use of Veterinarian locator search tool
- Access to all information on AMPA Website

- Newsletters for Members only
- AMPA Support
- Be a part of the movement to bridge gaps between owners, breeders, rescues, and veterinarians
- Access to AMPA ethical and reputable mini pig breeders directory
- Listing on the AMPA Membership Directory

Once you are a member, the next step is to register your mini pig. Registering your mini pig will place factual, verifiable data into the AMPA Registry Database. This is the first database of its kind in the history of mini pigs. By compiling data over the years, we will better understand growth, genetic issues, and the causes of death in these mini pigs. This will enable the community to work together for the betterment of the breed.

Be a part of history in the making by registering your mini pig as a pet in the AMPA registry! Join us to document true facts about mini pigs while scientifically establishing the American Mini Pig as a breed. When you add a registered piglet to your family from an AMPA Registered Breeder, your mini pig's lifetime registration is free for current AMPA Members.

Compiling reliable data will help to understand the genetics involved in mini pigs. We will be better able to predict mature size of offspring, to avoid potential health conditions, and provide important data to veterinarians that treat our mini pigs. A strong database will help to protect and advocate for pigs as pets.

AMPA Owner's Code of Ethics

Pig parents agree to love and commit to a good quality of life for all pigs.

Owner agrees to provide adequate housing.

- Indoor housing will include "pig-proofing" the house.

- Pigs are intelligent and strong and must root to be happy. Owners will recognize that this behavior can be destructive and will provide an area of safety for their pigs.

- Outdoor pigs will be provided with appropriate shelter (that protects from rain, snow, heat, sun).

- Outdoor pigs will have a safe fenced area or will be escorted on a harness and leash while outside. This is to protect from loss and from attack by stray dogs or hunters.

- Pigs will have fresh potable water at all times (unless there is a medical reason to remove the water).

-

Owners will protect their pig from other animals – Owners will be aware that even well socialized dogs can be hazardous to their pigs and will take appropriate action to prevent accidents from happening. Owners will also be aware that pigs can be a danger to other pets, and will take appropriate action to protect all of their pets.

Owner agrees to provide adequate veterinary care.

- Owners will have a regular daytime veterinarian prior to adoption.

- Owners will provide the pig with regular veterinary medical care including spay/neuter, vaccinations where appropriate, nutritional counseling, hoof care, dental care, parasite control, and skin care.

- Owners will research and find a veterinarian to use in case of an emergency.
- Owners will have animal poison control information handy.

Owner agrees to only adopt if home is zoned for a pet pig.

Owner agrees to license the pig (with city or county) when appropriate.

If the Owner is renting, owner will obtain written permission to have a pig prior to the adoption.

Owner agrees to become educated about the emotional, nutritional, financial, health, space, rooting, exercise requirements of pigs (before adopting). Owner agrees to continue to educate themselves during the life of their pig.

Owner agrees to provide the pig with a "forever home." If, due to unforeseen circumstances, owner must re-home the pig, the owner will work with the breeder to do so.

Owner agrees to provide an appropriate well-rounded structured diet. The owner agrees neither to over feed and cause obesity, nor to underfeed to keep the pig small. The body-shape scale should be used to determine proper size and body condition. Unless already done, Owner agrees to neuter or spay the pig (unless there is a medical reason not to do so)
Owner agrees to educate the general public about pigs whenever appropriate. The Owner agrees to act as an ambassador for the AMPA, and pet pigs in general, whenever possible.

Introduction

This handbook is a summary of basic information that can be helpful for new mini pig owners. This is by no means, everything you need to know about owning and caring for a mini pig. We have summarized and just scratched the surface of the basics. We recommended continuing education on the American Mini Pig Association website. We will be publishing a full version mini pig care book that will be available 2017.

We recommend finding support in mini pig Facebook groups, online forums, and by becoming a member of the AMPA. Your AMPA registered breeder will provide a lifetime of support. Never hesitate to ask questions.

The medical information you find in this handbook has been provided, reviewed, or approved by a mini pig vet. It does not and should not replace the advice of your own vet or replace the need for a veterinary appointment. It is provided for emergencies in the event that you cannot reach your vet or you cannot find a mini pig experienced vet. Please do not wait for an emergency or illness to find a vet for you pig. That should be among the first things you do for you new family member.

We hope that you find the information helpful. Remember to always be patient, have a sense of humor, be a consistent leader, and start training earlier to help create a lasting, respectful, loving, forever bond with your pig.

Chapter 1: Welcome to Pig Parenthood

Welcome to mini pig parenthood. We hope that with this handbook you can transition your new piglet into to your family feeling supported. Mini pigs are not naturally trusting animals and they are very aware of the dangers around them. It can take hours, days, or weeks before your mini pig is confident in its new surroundings. If your piglet is from an AMPA registered breeder then he/she has been weaned properly, and socialized prior to arriving. This will be extremely helpful to you as an owner and will make the experience more pleasant for your piglet and your family.

There are a number of items that you should have on hand to prepare for the arrival of your new family member.

Helpful Items

Every mini pig family will find the setup that works best for them. Not all pigs will need or enjoy the same items. When shopping for your piglet, consider the seasonal weather, whether s/he will be housed indoors or outdoors, where s/he will potty, how often you will travel or socialize, and how you plan to entertain your piglet. The following items are used by many mini pig parents:

- Bed and blankets

- Heavy food & water dish

- Pet playpen or baby gate to confine pig to a safe space

- Puppy potty pads or litter pan & litter such as horse bedding or pine pellets

- Kennel or Crate

- Veterinarian phone numbers
- Mini pig pelleted feed: Mazuri, Manna Pro, Purina, ask your breeder what brand they use

- Handy treats: Cheerios, dried fruits, infant puff snacks

- Figure 8 or A-Frame Harness & Leash

- First aid kit Available on AmericanMiniPigStore.com

What to Expect the First Night

The first night can be a scary time for a young piglet. Every piglet is an individual and may respond differently from being separated from the only family and home s/he has ever known. Some piglets adjust quickly and others need a bit of patience.

Your piglet should be at least 6 weeks old, weaned, and eating solid foods. Your AMPA Breeder has already started socializing your piglet and some have started on potty training. This effort helps to ensure a smooth transition for the piglet into your home and family.

The first day with your piglet will be very overwhelming to him/her. There is a whole world of new sights, sounds, and smells that s/he isn't used to. It is normal for your piglet to be fearful (lack of trust), jumpy, refuse to eat or drink, or to act aloof during the first 24 hours. Your piglet may be scared of fast movements, loud noises, other pets, or hands approaching. Do not force your piglet to be held or cause them any added stress during this crucial time.

Building Trust & Bond

Pigs are not born naturally social or trusting. Unlike a puppy, a piglet is not born tame. They are prey animals in the wild and instinctively will be nervous and want to flee as a response to movement, noise, or touch. Because of this, pigs require socialization and desensitization by the breeder or human in order to be pets.

Making sure a breeder spends a lot of time with their piglets gives an owner and a piglet a huge advantage in the socialization process. Often times if a breeder spends little to no time socializing their piglets, you will get a piglet that is skittish, squeals, screams, squirms, and bites. New owners do not know how to curb these behaviors. When bringing your mini pig home, you will notice that no matter how much your piglet has been socialized while with the breeder, they will still be a little scared and unsure of their new environment for the first few days or weeks in their new home. Piglets have just left their litter mates, parents, and caretakers for their first few months of life, which is all they know. They will need an ample amount of time, attention, and affection to get them to feel comfortable in their new home.

It is important to find a breeder that spends a lot of time socializing their piglets, and in turn shares how the piglet has been handled, and talked to. Your breeder can share how he or she holds the piglets, trains them, rewards them, and bonds with them so that you can mimic some of the same things making bonding and socialization process easier and more comforting to your piglet. Don't forget to talk and grunt to your pig. They will communicate with you often times mimicking your grunts, and you will both quickly learn what each other's sounds, tones, and your words mean. Pigs love to communicate and praise is a huge component to socializing and training.

When you bring your mini piglet home allow some time for the piglet or pig to adjust to its new surroundings and people. Pigs need some personal space at first and they need to know that the new people and the new home is safe. You can think of a pig more like a child instead of a pet in this case. If you had a new child in the house you would not smother them with hugs and kisses initially, it would take some time and you would give the child some space first and allow them to get comfortable.

A small area within the house or a pen will allow your pig to have its own space. Create a small enclosed place that includes their food bowl, heavy water bowl, litter box, and on the opposite side of the area their bed. Once a pig or piglet gets to know their surroundings, smells, voices, etc. slowly start getting to know your pig. Sit near your pig on their level so that they feel more comfortable. You can start introducing them to each family member to hold and spend time with, this could be a few hours or a full night or day. Pigs need to feel safe in their new environment and when being touched or held.

Some pigs are very social right off the bat, and others may need more time in the socialization process. Pigs need to feel confident and trusting of you before they are completely comfortable being pet and held. When being held, it is important that their back and front legs and/or neck/head is supported. Piglets get used to and prefer certain ways of being held, so if your breeder can send pictures or video of how they have been held it may be helpful. Most pigs like to be held tight against your chest.

If your piglet is too scared to be held comfortably, meaning they are squealing, biting, and/or trying to escape your arms, find a small space that can be blocked off and sit on the ground with them. Ground time is a great way to get your piglet to approach you, as sitting or lying on the ground makes you more approachable. You can use treats, such as Cheerios, and place one a few feet in front of you. Once your piglet responds to the treat continue putting down a treat slowly moving it in closer and closer to you. You want to do this frequently until your piglet is completely comfortable being touched by you.

Floor time creates trust and allows your piglet to feel comfortable approaching you without you trying to pick them up. A pig will back up when you try and reach for them, allow this floor time to be a time that your piglet can make the decision to come to you and freely approach you and eventually get on your lap, if smaller, without you grabbing for your pig. From there it will be much easier to slowly pick your piglet up and stand up. Pigs typically prefer to be picked up on the side of their body. Always reach from under the pig not over their bodies or heads.

For an older pig, the same exercise applies, you may just not be able to have it in your lap or stand up and hold your pig. After this training exercise is a continued success, your piglet should be much more comfortable being held by you and family members. Hold them on your chest or lap while you are watching television or include them in nap or bed time so they are comfortable falling asleep on you, get used to your smell, heartbeat, breathing, etc. The more holding and bonding time, the faster your pig will learn to trust and bond with you.

Chapter 2: Caring For Your Mini Pig

Housing

Mini pigs enjoy spending time indoors with their family. Piglets need a safe environment tailored to their specific & changing needs. When a new piglet is brought home, you will need to arrange for a small secure area where their basic needs are taken care of. Be careful not to give a piglet too much space at first. This is overwhelming, making it harder for them to trust you and to find their litter area. Starting out with a small space will give the piglet the chance to acclimate to the environment, connect with the people, and learn to use the litter box.

You can use a small room such as a bathroom for the first couple of days, a playpen, block off a small room with a baby gate, or use a puppy fence to create a small safe area. This area should have the piglet's non-tip water dish, litter box, bed, and blankets. Keep the litter box in the opposite side from the bedding. A crate is optional but very useful to teach the piglets to feel safe in crates. This will be vital training for later in life when the older pig needs transported to the veterinarian or for emergencies. As the piglet becomes acclimated you can give them more and more space, eventually giving them free run of the house.

Piglet proofing the home is important. Make sure any harmful chemicals or medications are far out of reach. Pigs will tear into any container or cabinet that they think may have food of any sort. Keep cat food, dog food, and pig's food secure and out of reach. You may need pantry locks or fridge locks to keep pigs out. Purses, backpacks, and other bags should be kept off the ground and out of reach.

Protecting your piglet from other household pets and vice versa is very important. At this age your piglet isn't a threat to most other pets, but dogs can and have killed piglets when least expected. Keep your piglet separated from your dog(s) when you are not supervising. As your pig matures, s/he may become a threat to your other pets. Keep a watchful eye and don't tolerate any aggressive behavior. If pets do not get along, keep them separated.

Housing mini pigs outdoors is as simple as weather protection, predator protection, and strong fencing. Plenty of fresh water should be available at all times in a non-tippable container. Kiddie pools are a great choice to provide drinking water and also a place for the mini pig to cool off in hot weather.

Pigs should be given as much space as possible outdoors, but only in areas where they are allowed to act like pigs. Some pigs have more rooting drive than others, but they can usually be counted on to ruin the most prized landscaping. If you have areas of grass or landscaping that you want to protect from your mini pig, be sure to fence the area off. Standard wooden fencing or chain-link fencing work well for most spayed and neutered mini pigs. Some pigs, most especially intact pigs looking for love, are quite persistent in their escape efforts. They will break through or root under the fencing. The strongest fencing and most appropriate fencing for mini pigs is cattle panel. These 16-foot-long metal fencing panels can be found at Tractor Supply or any farm store. They can be used to fence in an entire yard or build a smaller "pen" for your mini pig in your yard.

Your mini pig will need protection from the weather and predators. In city areas, loose dogs are the biggest threat to pet pigs. In rural areas there may be other predators. At the very least, strong fencing and shelter will be needed to protect your pig. Shelters should protect from wind, rain, flooding, sun, and snow.

Parasite Control – Deworming

Pigs should be dewormed on a regular basis for internal and external parasites. These parasites are common in the pig's environment, especially those that root and graze or spend time outdoors. Mini pigs can contract parasites from soil, grazing, other pigs, other pets, eating bugs (including earth worms or mealworms), or contact with hay. Even if pig parents have horses or work in a barn they can bring parasites to their indoor pigs. Most of these parasites will show no symptoms until after they have taken a toll on your pig's health. Many of the parasites will not show up on a fecal exam.

A regular schedule of two broad spectrum dewormers will kill the internal and external parasites your pigs are prone to carrying. Pigs should be dewormed every 4-6 months depending on your area. Two easily accessible and easily dosed dewormers that will cover the common parasites found in pet pigs are ivermectin (brand name Ivomec or Noromectin) and fenbendazole (brand name Safe-guard).

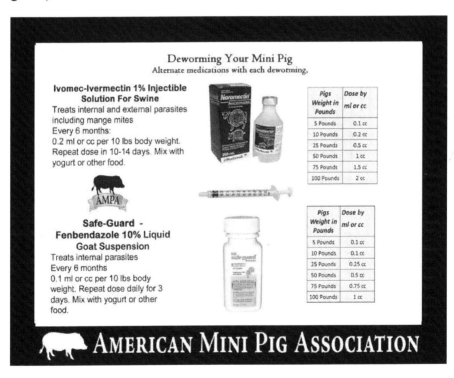

Deworming Your Mini Pig
Alternate medications with each deworming,

Ivomec-Ivermectin 1% Injectible Solution For Swine
Treats internal and external parasites including mange mites
Every 6 months:
0.2 ml or cc per 10 lbs body weight.
Repeat dose in 10-14 days. Mix with yogurt or other food.

Pigs Weight in Pounds	Dose by ml or cc
5 Pounds	0.1 cc
10 Pounds	.0.2 cc
25 Pounds	0.5 cc
50 Pounds	1 cc
75 Pounds	1.5 cc
100 Pounds	2 cc

Safe-Guard - Fenbendazole 10% Liquid Goat Suspension
Treats internal parasites
Every 6 months
0.1 ml or cc per 10 lbs body weight. Repeat dose daily for 3 days. Mix with yogurt or other food.

Pigs Weight in Pounds	Dose by ml or cc
5 Pounds	0.1 cc
10 Pounds	0.1 cc
25 Pounds	0.25 cc
50 Pounds	0.5 cc
75 Pounds	0.75 cc
100 Pounds	1 cc

AMERICAN MINI PIG ASSOCIATION

Socializing

Anytime you are holding, praising, training, or spending time with your mini pig you are socializing them to humans. Slowly including family members and visitors in this will help get them comfortable with others within the home. When introducing your pig and children, make sure they children are calm. Piglets will get startled by loud noise or running or chasing, a good first introduction is key with pigs and children.

When introducing strangers start slowly and allow the pig to be around the new family member before they are held. Ground time for strangers and talking to them first and allowing the pig to approach will give your pig freedom and help build confidence. Taking them for car rides and places with you as well as introducing them to strangers in and out of the home, is great socialization for your piglet. Pigs that are only in the home, or pigs that are not introduced to new people can grow increasingly leery of strangers and visitors especially as they get older. If you do not want a timid pig, spend as much time as possible getting them comfortable with others.

Outdoor Time & Enrichment

Mini pigs do best with daily time spent outdoors. Outdoor excursions allow them to be a pig! Spending time outdoors will benefit the pig's health and behavior. Healthy pigs will need about 15 minutes of sunlight daily for proper Vitamin D3 absorbency. Mini pigs also root in the dirt to acquire essential minerals such as iron and selenium. This outdoor time gives the pigs an outlet for their natural behaviors such as rooting, grazing, and foraging. Restricting mini pigs to indoors only often causes several behavioral problems due to boredom. Many pet pigs enjoy the life of luxury living and sleeping inside, but still need daily outdoor time to thrive.

Animal enrichment is the process of providing a stimulating environment for your pet. Enrichment is described as improving or enhancing the environment to provide an outlet for natural behaviors and needs through physical and mental challenges. These types of enrichment are used by zoos, sanctuaries, and pet owners worldwide. Enrichment is essential to a healthy and happy pet. You are likely already providing enrichment every day to your pig without realizing it. By understanding pig's natural behaviors, you can create activities for him to enrich his life and meet his needs.

Pigs are incredibly sensitive and intelligent animals. This high level of intelligence can be challenging in a home environment. Pigs require physical and mental stimulation to meet their needs. A busy pig is a happy pig! Keeping a pig contained to a crate or alone in a room all day with no companionship or stimulation is sure to create a bored, agitated, destructive, and possibly aggressive pig. By using activities to enrich their lives (with or without you) you can avoid many unhealthy behaviors while building a better bond with your pig. Enrichment helps to provide the life your pig deserves.

Enrichment activities offer an outlet for natural behaviors. Daily routines are the perfect opportunity for enrichment. Instead of feeding in a bowl, pig feed can be sprinkled throughout the yard for foraging. Instead of giving vitamins/supplements, the pig can do a few tricks and then rewarded with the vitamins. Enrichment is open ended fun. Get creative, get interactive, have fun!

Enrichment activities should be interesting, challenging, and novel. Enrichment should be used every day with your pig, although the complexity will vary. This is one area routine is not preferred. Switch it up, keep it interesting, and always challenging.

Types of enrichment may include physical exercise, mental exercise, training or interactions with the human family, olfactory using scents, auditory using sounds, food related, novel objects, exploring new environments or manipulating the home environment.

Visit the www.AmericanMiniPigAssociation.com for enrichment ideas or find us on Pinterest.

Grinding Teeth

Pigs grind their teeth for a variety of reasons. To determine why your pig is grinding you'll want to pay attention to their overall behavior, body language, the length and timing of the teeth grinding.

- Teething
- Pain
- Stress or Agitation
- Contentment (Piggy Purrs)
- Boredom

Teething is obviously uncomfortable. Pigs get 3 sets of teeth in their lives. Piglets will start getting some grind-worthy teeth in near 4 months old. Around a year old some of these teeth will loosen and fall out. The loose-toothed grind is particularly challenging to our ears. It can sound like they are chewing rocks! Once the loose teeth fall out, they may grind again as the new teeth erupt. Grinding puts pressure on the gums which provides counter pressure and relief for the pain of the emerging teeth. You'll notice when they grind for emerging teeth it will make a squeaky noise as the gums (instead of teeth) are rubbing together. If your pig's teeth grinding is persistent for two weeks without any other signs of distress, it's probably caused by teething. This type of teeth grinding should subside by 2 years old.

You can give a mild pain reliever for short term relief, but it really just needs to run its course. Some pig parents will give their pigs Whimzees, which are similar to Greenies dog chews but are said to have safer ingredients. You can also make frozen treats for your piggy with yogurt, pumpkin, peanut butter, fruit juice, or other healthy foods. Freeze in ice cube trays or silicone molds. Frozen apple slices or frozen veggies.

A pig in physical pain may grind in the way we would clench our jaws or hands. If the teeth grinding is accompanied by other pain signals, then you may want to visit the vet to ensure everything is ok with your porcine pal. Your pig could have an abscess or something stuck in the teeth. If the grinding persists, try to check their teeth for any abnormalities or schedule a visit with the veterinarian. If your pig goes off his feed, there is a problem your vet will need to assess.

Mini pigs will grind their teeth from stress or agitation. If you made your piggy mad they will tell you! This is a firm and deliberate grind. This will be louder than other grinds and sound more forceful. Instead of rubbing it will sound like clashing. Pigs will do this if they are annoyed, stressed, or agitated. Pig introductions can certainly trigger some angry teeth grinds or even chomps! Moving furniture or changing routine can trigger stress in your pig. If your pig's teeth grinding is accompanied by other piggy-tantrum behaviors, you can assume it's agitation causing the grinding. Special treats or quiet one on one time may help your pig feel a bit more comforted.

Contentment is the best form of teeth grinding, affectionately referred to as Piggy Purrs. You will know they are purring because their body will be completely relaxed, not a care in the world. This grinding is very rhythmic and soothing. The piglet may be getting a belly rub or a good scratch while laying on their favorite human. No cure for this happy grinding, just enjoy it.

It's been said pigs will grind their teeth out of boredom, similar to a person fidgeting with their fingers. If you suspect your pig is grinding from boredom, offer some stimulating activities. Instead of feeding out of a bowl, feed from a treat ball or sprinkle food around the room or the yard, or in a rooting box, or in a pile of clothes.

Pain Relief for Teething

- Ice cubes

- Frozen treats - Coconut oil, yogurt, peanut butter, canned pumpkin, juice, any mix
- Whimzees (dog chew, similar to Greenies)

Hooves & Tusks

Hooves and tusks will not need to be maintained until your piglet is much older. It's important to understand this very basic care routine in order to prepare and plan ahead.

Hooves are a very basic part of caring for your mini pig. Most pig owners choose to care for hooves at home. It is also acceptable to take your pig to the veterinarian to maintain hooves, although this is the costlier option. Whichever routine you choose, it's in the best interest of your mini pig to get him used to having his hooves handled from a very young age. Play with your pig's feet and hooves on a daily basis to desensitize him to having them handled. By getting him used to having his feet handled, he will allow you to trim his hooves without restraint or anesthesia. In a young pig, a human nail file or fingernail clipper will do the job. As the piglet gets older, the hooves will become much bigger and harder. Then you'll want to switch to heavier tools. Goat hoof trimmers, rose pruning shears, and dremel tools are all used by mini pig parents. Trim nails as often as necessary to maintain proper length. The longer the hooves grow, the harder it will be to trim them back to a healthy length. Failure to maintain hooves can result in severely overgrown hooves, pain, arthritis, and eventual disability in the pig. It would take years of neglect to reach this point, but it's always better to trim too often than not often enough. Help your mini pig keep hooves naturally maintained by taking walks or placing paving stones or concrete in his pen area. Walking on these hard surfaces will cause the friction needed to maintain the hoof length requiring less trims.

All mini pigs grow tusks eventually. These usually do not show up until after the pig is a year old, sometimes closer to two years old. Most parents don't recognize tusks for what they are until they have grown quite a bit longer than the other teeth. Tusk removal is not recommended as these special ivory teeth are part of the jawbone, they do not have "roots" like the other teeth that can be pulled out. Females do have tusks, although they may never grow long enough to be visible past the lip line. Male tusks will grow longer and faster. Intact boars have the fastest tusk growth. Barrows, neutered males, will most likely need their tusks trimmed at some point, but not until they are several years old. It's a personal preference on tusk length. Some prefer the naturally longer tusks, while others are concerned with safety of humans and other pets by accidental tusking. In some cases, pig's tusks are growing at a bad angle and will turn back towards the face of the mini pig. If not trimmed, these tusks can cause great pain and damage as they grow into the skull. Tusk trimming is a very simple and quick procedure done by a veterinarian. A gigli wire will be used to saw the tusk off at the appropriate level. This may be done with or without anesthesia, depending on your veterinarian's preferences.

Keep in mind, anesthesia in mini pigs is very expensive and in some cases dangerous. Work with your piglet to have his feet and teeth handled without fear. This will make routine care much easier for the years you will spend together, and also safer. Keep your mini pig at a healthy weight. Obesity causes great additional risks when anesthesia is used.

Skin & Hair Care

Skin and hair care is easy in mini pigs. Most pigs don't need baths, but if you choose to bathe your piglet use a mild soap or shampoo. Baby shampoo or Mane N Tail shampoo and conditioner will keep your piglet's skin and hair soft and healthy. Do not bath too often or use scented lotions that can irritate skin. Products made for babies or sensitive skin should be ok for your mini pig.

Diet is a large part of skin and hair health. Keep your mini pig on a balanced diet with the addition of selenium, vitamin e, biotin, and healthy fats such as coconut oil to build healthy skin and hair from within.

Mini pigs do not shed on a regular basis but they do blow their coats typically on a yearly basis. During this seasonal change they will shed all of their hair and grow back a new coat of hair. The first coat blow is usually during the summer after their first birthday. Coat blowing also causes dry, itchy, irritated skin. Give extra attention to brushing and moisturizing during this time. To help speed the process and make your pig more comfortable you may gently pull the loose hairs off.

Dippity Pig Syndrome

Written by Cathy Corrigan, DVM

Dippity Pig Syndrome, also called Bleeding Back Syndrome and Erythema Multiforme, is an acute, painful skin condition that occurs along the back in healthy young pigs.

Symptoms:

Occurs in young pigs – between 4 months and 4 years

Sudden, rapid onset

Screaming/squealing in pain

Dipping or temporary loss of use of hind legs – it usually does not affect front legs

Red, oozing sores on back – there are usually more than one, and they make stripes across the back rather than following the length of the back bone

Pigs will try to run or move away from the pain

Pigs will usually eat and drink

Pigs will usually have normal stool and urine

Pigs will usually have a normal body temperature

Usually lasts 2-4 days

Can reoccur in some pigs

Happens most often in small pet pigs, occasionally in show pigs, and has been reported a few times in farm pigs

Seems to be associated with a stressful situation

Cause:

The cause of Dippity Pig Syndrome is not known. There is some evidence, based on biopsy results, that it may involve a herpes virus (like shingles in the human being). There is evidence that it occurs in some family lines.

Treatment:

This condition will resolve after 2-4 days with no medical intervention

Reduce stress in the environment – keep the pig in a quite familiar environment with soft bedding, dim light, soft music and reduced noise.

Isolate the pig from people – these pigs are very painful. In some cases, even blowing on their backs will cause a collapse. They need to be left alone to rest.

Some veterinarians will use anti-inflammatory steroids to treat Dippity. NSAIDs have also been used. Since there is some evidence that a herpes virus may be involved, this treatment is somewhat controversial.

For pain:

Buffered aspirin, 5 mg per pound every 12 hours, with a meal. For no more than 3 days
OR
Tylenol, 5 mg per pound every 8 hours. (If you use infant's Tylenol, 1 cc per 6 pounds). Always with food. For no more than 3 days
Tramadol or buprenex can be prescribed by your veterinarian for pain control.

To help the pig rest:

Benadryl (aka diphenhydramine) up to 1 mg per pound every 8 hours.

REASONS TO HAVE YOUR PIG SEEN BY A VETERINARIAN:

If you are worried about him/her

If the pig is not responding to treatment

If the condition continues for longer than 4 days

If both the back AND front legs are involved (probably not Dippity)

If your pig will not eat nor drink

If your pig continues to be very painful

If your pig runs a fever (temperature greater than 103)

If your pig seems unresponsive

Finding a Veterinarian

Mini pig parents are often surprised by how many veterinarians do not treat their pets. Always setup a veterinarian before you bring your mini pig home. It's also a good idea to have a back up veterinarian and an emergency veterinarian for the worst timed scenarios.

Find a mini pig veterinarian near you at www.AMPAvets.com

Emergency Medical Care

Mini Pig Emergency Medical Information written by Dr. Cathy Corrigan, DVM.

If your pig is sick, go to a veterinarian. Do not try to treat the pig yourself.

Murphy's law of veterinary medicine: Your pig will get sick at night, on a holiday, or after hours.

Reasons to go to the ER now:

- Your pig will not eat

- Your pig will not move

- Your pig is shaking violently, is stiff, or is moving in circles, has a head tilt

- Your pig is having trouble breathing

- Your pig is vomiting blood or having bloody diarrhea

- Your pig's body temperature is below 99 or above 104

- Your pregnant pig has been pushing hard for 1 hour, you can see a piglet or part of a piglet in the vaginal canal, but the piglet is not coming

Things to have on hand, to help your pig UNTIL you get to the veterinarian:

Strawberry Koolaid – for pigs who do not want to drink, or have low blood sugar. Can be used to give some meds since it can mask the taste of a bitter compound

Gatorade(regular/original) or pedialyte – balanced electrolyte solutions to replace fluid lost if vomiting or diarrhea occur.

Low sodium chicken broth – can be used to replace fluid lost if vomiting or diarrhea occur

Campbell's vegetable soup – many pigs will eat this when it is warmed up when they will not eat anything else.

Canned pumpkin – high fiber to help if constipation or diarrhea occur

Applesauce – many pigs will eat this when they have poor appetite. Can be used to hide medication

Heating pad – for the cold pig. Set on low so piggie doesn't get burned. Also adds security for new pigs – they sleep better on those first nights home.

Karo syrup – a sugar source to help very cold or inappetant pigs

Sugar – 1 teaspoonful in a cup of warm water can be put on gums to raise blood sugar of cold pigs. They do not have to drink it, it can be absorbed through the mucous membranes of the lips and gums.

Instant oatmeal – many pigs will eat warm oatmeal when they do not eat anything else

A few syringes of different sizes or a turkey baster so that you can give liquids orally

A digital thermometer – to be used rectally (get one for only pig use)

A fan for cooling

Ice packs(or frozen peas in a bag) for cooling and in case of a injury to a leg. Put a small towel between the ice pack and the skin.

Honey – a sugar source for cold pigs – rub some on the gums. Can also be mixed in with canned pumpkin if they are reluctant to eat it

Full spectrum light (SAD light) – can be obtained online. Provides sunlight for pigs that are indoors only – needed so that Vitamin D can be produced and used. 10 minutes per day. Especially useful for piglets

Kwik Stop – a styptic powder to help bleeding hooves if you quick them during trimming. DO NOT USE ON SKIN because it can burn the tissue

Super glue – if you quick a claw during trimming, you can glue a cotton ball onto bleeding area and it will stop. Cotton will fall off or can be removed later

Q-tips & KY jelly or Vaseline (or both) – can be used to lubricate and moisten tissue. A small amount on a q-tip can be used to clean the outside of the ear

Handy bandage material (in case of a cut, scrape, etc):

Disposable diapers or sanitary napkins – clean absorbent material, easy to store and always have about.

Masking tape (does not stick to skin, but sticks to bandage material)

A couple of pairs of athletic socks or some boots made for dogs – to cover feet

1 inch white bandage tape, rolled gauze and vetwrap

ASPCA NATIONAL ANIMAL POISON CONTROL (available 24 hours a day) There is a fee, so have credit card ready   1-800-548-2423

Please contact your local ER vets before you have an emergency, so you know where to take your pigs if you need emergency care.

Helpful over-the-counter drugs to have on hand:

For Upset Stomach (vomiting, not eating, diarrhea)

Omprazole / Prilosec – 5-10 mg once a day

Famotidine / Pepcid – 0.25-0.5 mg per pound of bodyweight

Ranitidine / Zantac – 150 mg twice a day

Pepto bismol – 1 cc per pound of body weight – may make the stool black

Kaopectate – 1 cc per pound of body weight – may make the stool black

Maalox liquid (for stomach gas) – 2 cc per 5 pounds of body weight

For Pain:

Buffered aspirin – 5 mg per pound of body weight twice a day. Must be buffered and given with food. Do not give if your pig is not eating and do not give for more than 3days without seeing your vet.

Many people have asked about liquid ibuprofen children's syrup (also called brufen liquid). I know that this compound is frequently used in the UK, but I was unable to find a recommended dose in the US. As a matter of fact, pharmacologists in the US uniformly advise against use of ibuprofen, acetominophin, advil, motrin, Tylenol, etc., in pigs. As such, I have not added these to my list.

For Constipation: (need high fiber diet)

Metamucil – start with 1 tbsp power in yogurt every 6 hours. Gradually build up to 1 packet every 6 hours

DSS / docusate sodium (stool softener) – 200-240 mg per pig twice a day

Fleet enema

Mineral oil (can be given orally or rectally)

If no significant stool in 48 hours, see vet

For Itching / Hives / Swollen Eyes

Diphenhydramine / Benadryl – 1 mg per pound of body weight every 6-8 hours.

For Weeping Eyes:

Saline eye flush

Terramycin ophthalmic ointment (available at feed store). Put a small amount in each eye twice a day

To Kill Many Parasites:

Ivermectin 1% injectable (or oral) 10 mg/ml . 0.1 – 0.2 ml per 10 pounds of body weight. Mix in yogurt or fruit juice and they will slurp it right down.

For Coughing Pigs:

Children's cough syrup – (dextromethorphan 15 mg per 10 ml) – 10 ml per pig twice a day.

For Pigs that have Ingested Poison:

Call poison control 800-548-2423 (ASPCA NATIONAL ANIMAL POISON CONTROL – available 24 hours a day) There is a fee, so have credit card ready

Hydrogen Peroxide 3% (in the brown bottle, for wounds) – can be given orally (by syringe) to induce vomiting

Dose: approximately 5cc per 10 pounds of body weight

Activated charcoal – adheres to any toxin left in the digestive tract and prevents pig from absorbing it – get the liquid or powdered form (the tablets/granules are not nearly as effective). Watch out – this stuff is messy and will stain anything. Comes out in the stool and the stool will also stain everything. Dose: adult pigs (over 30 pounds – 0.5 ml per pound of body weight) young pigs (less than 30 pounds – 0.1 ml per pound of body weight. Can be repeated in 8 hours.

Warning – vomiting is not always good after a pig ingests a poison. Call poison control or your ER first

Chapter 3: Nutrition & Healthy Weight

Healthy Foods

Most fruits, vegetable, and unprocessed foods that we enjoy are also healthy for mini pigs. Moderation and variety is always recommended. While a food may be safe to eat, too much of a good thing can cause issues. Excess sugar, even in fruits, contributes to dangerous obesity and dental rot. Consider overall calorie intake when choosing foods for your mini pigs. The majority of the diet should be vegetables with lots of leafy greens, mini pig pellets as appropriate, and small occasional portions of fruits, grains, cereals, nuts, seeds, or supplements.

See Appendix 1 for a list of healthy fruits, vegetables, nuts and seeds, and grains.

Healthy Pelleted Diet

Mini pigs do very well on a commercial pelleted diet. These have been nutritionally balanced for the needs of a mini pig. Follow the guidelines on the package label for portion sizes and adjust to the needs of your pig to keep him at a healthy weight.

In addition to pellets, mini pigs should be given the opportunity to graze, root, and offered plenty of healthy vegetables. Pigs are naturally omnivores eating a variety of foods. Try to include as much nutritional variety for your pig in the produce department. Leafy green vegetables, root vegetables, summer squash, winter squash, and vegetables of all different colors each provide nutritional variety.

Mini pigs love to eat! They are very food driven, giving the impression that they are hungry all the time. As cute as they are, it's important to not overfeed. Feeding mini pigs the correct portions is important for their long term health. Overfeeding and underfeeding are both dangerous and will damage the health of your mini pig, shortening their lifespan.

There is no amount of food that is appropriate for all mini pigs. Every pig should be fed according to their own individual needs. It is ok to use guidelines as a starting point. Then, periodically asses your mini pig to ensure he is at the proper body condition. If he starts looking too thin, then increase the feed until he levels out. If he starts to look too round you need to decrease the amount of pellets he is getting. Grazing can add a lot of weight. If your pig is grazing, he will need less pellets.

Dr. Cathy Corrigan recommends ¼ cup of mini pig pellets twice per day for every 25 lbs. weight as a starting point. Alternately, mini pigs should be fed 2% of their body weight in feed. To calculate this amount, you will need to weigh the food with a kitchen scale to determine the volume of the specified weight of your mini pig's food. If you do not have a scale, you can estimate food weight at ½ lb. = 1 cup.

To calculate the measurement to feed, multiply your pig's weight by 0.02. This equation will give you the weight in lbs. that your pig should be fed per day.

For example, a 50 lb. pig would be fed 1 lb. per day.

Lbs. pig weight x 2% = Lbs. of food per day

50 (lbs. pig) x 0.02 (2%) = 1 lb. food

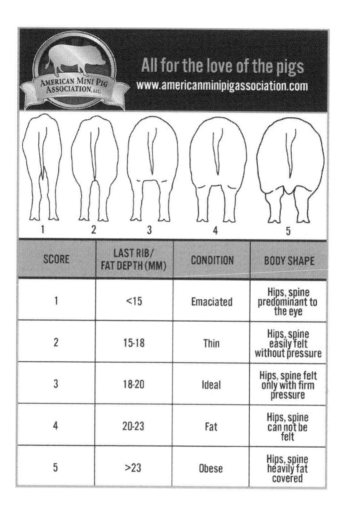

<table>
</table>

SCORE	LAST RIB/ FAT DEPTH (MM)	CONDITION	BODY SHAPE
1	<15	Emaciated	Hips, spine predominant to the eye
2	15-18	Thin	Hips, spine easily felt without pressure
3	18-20	Ideal	Hips, spine felt only with firm pressure
4	20-23	Fat	Hips, spine can not be felt
5	>23	Obese	Hips, spine heavily fat covered

Healthy Treats

The way to a pig's heart is food! Treats are great for training and bonding with mini pigs. When offering treats, choose low calorie, low sugar, healthy treats. Overindulgence in treats can lead to unhealthy weight gain and behavioral problems (Spoiled Pig Syndrome). A great training technique is to use the mini pig's pellets for a training session instead of feeding in a bowl. It's a great workout physically and mentally.

Order the AMPA Mini Pig Cookbook full of recipes for frozen treats, cookies, cakes, natural diet, skin care, bug repellents, urine removers, and first aid.

www.AmericanMiniPigStore.com

Whole grain cereals – Cheerios, Shredded Wheat
Vegetables – squash, zucchini, eggplant, cherry tomatoes, etc
Dehydrated or dried fruits or vegetables
Raisins
Dried Cranberries
Gerber Toddler Puffs
Granola
Peanut Butter on celery
Popcorn Air Popped
(No oils, butter, or seasoning)
100% Pumpkin Canned
Eggs – Scrambled, hardboiled, or raw

Chapter 4: Behavior & Training

Introducing Piglet to Other Pets

When introducing to other house pets, start slowly and watch for body language. A dog should be leashed or behind a baby gate when first introducing. Pigs are social animals. They thrive around other animals and they need companionship, so pets are a very important part of your pig's life. It is important that you trust the interaction between your piglet and said pets before ever leaving them alone together.

Many breeders recommend NEVER leaving your pig alone with dogs or other pets that can potentially hurt or attack your pig. Owners need to know their pets well and make decisions on when is a good time to allow them to run together and whether or not they can ever be together while supervised or alone.

Introducing Piglet to Older Pigs

Pigs are herd animals that enforce a strict hierarchy with herd mates. Adding a pig to the family can result in some temporary upset. The pig's first meeting may result in a fight. In addition, established pigs may be extra grumpy or snippy with their family while they get settled with the new family addition.

Piglets should be introduced to older pigs carefully. In most situations, there will be a challenge by the older pig. It's important to protect the piglet from harm, although this is a completely natural interaction for pigs and usually there is no harm done.

The least stressful way to introduce piglets is to use the barrier method. Keep the established pig and piglet separated by a fence or baby gate. Allow them to see and smell each other, but unable to hurt each other. There may be aggressive posturing, teeth chomping, foaming, pacing back and forth, mohawks, or charging the fence. This is ok as long as they are securely separated. Keep them separated as long as this lasts. It could be a day or two weeks. Let the pig's set the timeline.

Once the pigs are not reacting to each other at all, you can remove the barrier. Their first introduction needs to be in a wide open space where they can get good footing. An outdoor fenced area is preferable. You can smear Vaseline on the pig's ears to protect them from bites or scratches. On initial introduction, the older pig may charge, chase, or bite at the piglet. The piglet's defense to this is to RUN fast to get out of the older pig's way. This retreat will show submission to the established pig. If the floor is slippery or if furniture is in the way, then the piglet will not be able to retreat as needed. This will cause more fighting and possibly injuries. This show of submission is necessary for the pigs to come to an understanding within the herd hierarchy. Once this is settled the pigs will quickly become best of friends!

Remember the scuffles are perfectly natural. Take it slow to avoid unnecessary stress and injury. If the scuffle is mild, do not interfere! The established pig needs to make it clear to the piglet that he is the dominant leader. This is the way pigs communicate. They will get it worked out and become lifelong friends. Continue to feed the pigs separately as long as necessary to ensure the younger piglet is getting his fair share of food.

Spoiled Pig Syndrome (SPS)

Spoiled Pig Syndrome refers to the behavioral problems of a pet pig that does not respect his humans. It's all about respect, but you have to earn it! Spoiled pigs quickly become accustomed to getting what they want, when they want it. When they don't get their way, they will act out. These tantrums and fits of anger can result in dangerous aggressive behavior. When a pig becomes spoiled, everyone is miserable, including the pig. Set boundaries, enforce them, and enjoy a relaxed relationship with your mini pig built on trust and respect.

Pigs become spoiled when they are overindulged or not given adequate leadership structure. In a household, when the pig does not respect the people as leaders, they will treat them as lower ranking herd members. Pigs live in a world of very strict hierarchy. The leader reinforces their role often throughout the day. In a group of pigs, the herd leader will not tolerate misbehavior from pigs of lower ranking. Leader pigs are quick to correct the lower ranking pigs, swift and stern. Lower ranking pigs quickly react to the orders of the herd leader, or face the consequences. To live happily with a pet pig, you need to be the herd leader. Do not allow yourself to become the "lower ranking pig".

If the pig demands food by rooting at your leg while you are cooking, and you give him a bite, he has become higher ranking than you and expect you to follow his orders. If you fail to do as the pig wants, he will "correct" you with swift and sternness. When you feed your pig to quiet them when they are screaming, you are shifting the leadership role to your pig and telling them it's ok to set demands for you to fulfill. If you feed your pig snacks often throughout the day, he will start to expect and demand food.

When food isn't available he will become frustrated and angry.

Signs of Spoiled Pig Syndrome (SPS):

- Screaming
- Biting
- Charging
- Growling
- Snapping
- Head Swiping
- Snatching Food
- Failure to move when asked
- Destructive Behaviors (angrily shredding bedding, furniture, or other items)

How to Prevent & Correct Spoiled Pig Syndrome:

- Nothing is Free – Every morsel of food needs to be worked for. Ask the pig to sit or spin before offering the treat. Nothing is free, it should all be earned.
- Restrict food to mealtimes – If pigs are expecting food at all hours of the day and night, they will demand it. To rein in a spoiled pig, restrict food to mealtimes only, 2 or 3 times a day. Do NOT feed your pig a bite of food when you are preparing meals, do not feed out of the kitchen, do not give the pig a bite when you are eating, do not feed the pig off your plate. There needs to be a very clear distinction of their food vs your food, so they are not expecting food unless it is actually intended for them.
- Work the Mind – Instead of feeding out of bowls, have your pig work for their food. Scatter food throughout the yard or spend 10-15 minutes in a training session while they earn each bite of their food. The more time you spend training your mini pig, the better you will be able to communicate with each other. Just 10 to 15 minutes once or twice a day will give you plenty of opportunity to interact, learn, and teach. Besides the basic commands like

sit, stay, bow, you are also learning together how to communicate with each other. Positive rewards will have them yearning to learn more and do as you've asked.

- Move The Pig (MTP) – Practice MTP throughout the day, at all different times of the day, for no particular reason. When you choose, walk up to your pig and expect them to move out of your way, out of the kitchen, off their bed, off the porch, off the couch, or out of the hallway. This is classic leadership communication between pigs. MTP earns respect and reinforces hierarchy boundaries.

- Outdoor Time – Make sure your pig gets plenty of outdoor time daily. Housebound pigs are far more likely to develop Spoiled Pig Syndrome symptoms.

- Expect Respect – Set yourself up as the herd leader, enforce the rules, and expect respect. If your pig snaps or swipes you need to correct them. Do not tolerate misbehavior or acts of aggression, no matter how small it seems. Those little seeds of disrespect grow and fester into bigger problems that are more difficult to correct.

- Routine – Mini pigs thrive on routine. Setup a clear routine for your mini pig that he can depend on. Pre-mealtime routines are particularly helpful in combating spoiled pigs. Instead of having a screaming pig at your feet while you prepare a salad, keep the pig out of the kitchen until the meal is ready. Before you feed, ask him to do a series of tricks. Go to a particular mat and sit, then spin, wave, and bow. THEN, put the food bowl down for him to eat his lunch. Continue this routine with each meal and he will look forward to earning that meal. Instead of being frantic and hysterical for food, he will be THINKING about the moves he's learned to get what he wants.

Understanding Behaviors

Pigs have complex social structures and communication. To communicate with each other, they use body language, vocal communications, and scent/pheromones. Our sense of smell cannot pick up most of their species specific signals, so we focus more on the body and vocal cues.

Vocalizations can be grunts, squeals, barks, huffs, "hot panting", screams, arfs, and a whole lot that are hard to type! Body Language includes posture, movement, lack of movement, direction of movement, expressions, head movements, physical contact, closeness, eye contact, etc.

Vocalizations

Pigs vocalize for all the same reasons we do. If they are happy, sad, lonely, hurt, scared, hungry, demanding, submitting, challenging, warning, terrified, making friends, greeting friends or family, searching for friends, mourning, excited, bored, bonding, enjoying company, warning family members of danger, agitated or quite simply content. They have distinct vocalizations for pain, stress, food anticipation, farrowing (giving birth), nursing (they call their babies for milk and sing to them as they nurse), they vocalize when they are in heat, greeting a mate, when they are isolated or startled. Several studies have been done to understand and evaluate swine vocalizations that also apply to our mini pigs. Often times, vocalizations alone will only tell you so much. Combine the vocalizations with the body language, environment, and other tell-tale signs coming from the pig to put together the whole picture.

In general, high pitched vocalizations are stress related while low pitched vocalizations are comfortable/relaxed communications between loved ones. A pig that whines, screeches or shrills is not happy (stress, agitation, challenging). A pig that coos or grunts rhythmically is content and relaxed surrounded by those he trusts and loves.

Angry, Agitated, or Aggressive Vocalizations:

- Jaw chomping or clacking
- Teeth grinding (can also be a pleasant response)
- Screeching with a shrill tone as if the pig is screeching AT you, forcefully telling you something
-

Happy, Excited or Content Vocalizations:

- Grunting: Pigs grunt to greet each other, talk to their piglets, communicate with loved ones, and simply to chatter about their day. This is a very content communication, as they chat and bond.

- Oof Oof or Ahh Ahhh Ahhh: Greeting that can sound like laughing or "monkey noises". This is a mellow, soft sound. It's not particularly loud, it does not have sharp tones or fluctuations. It's a level noise that they seem to push out with effort to greet their loved ones. If you get this greeting, consider yourself CHERISHED! My pigs do this often if we've been apart for several hours and they get excited to see me again.

- Hot panting: This is another family greeting pigs offer to their most trusted family members. They will come close to you, or a body part such as a foot, and huff huff huff blowing hot air on you. They are adorable when they curl their lips just-so. The body language shows a pig completely at ease and relaxed. He has full trust in you and enjoys your companionship.

- Teeth grinding (can also be a response to pain or agitation). Pigs often grind their teeth when they are relaxing and content. Pay attention to the timing and body language. Is it meal time? Is he pacing? Are his eyes darting around the room? Is he starting at his arch nemesis (another pet? a person?) He's not happy. Is he getting a belly rub or snuggled up under your favorite comforter? Then he's very happy.... My little Olivia would grind her teeth when she was very tired. I didn't feel it was a stress response, but that she was self-comforting to sooth herself to sleep.

Fear or Stress Vocalizations:

- Screaming: These have been recorded at decibels rivaling a jet engine. Pigs and piglets will squeal/scream "at the top of their lungs" from pain or fear. When a pig screams from pain or fear, he will also try to get away from the trigger. His body language will be tense, his movements will be quick, jerky, sporadic (think of a chipmunk). He is in extreme distress and feels as if he is fighting for his life. If given the chance, he will flee and will elude capture to the best of his abilities. There is no mistaking this noise, or what it means. The typical questions is "How do I stop my pig from screaming?". The easy answer is: take away the trigger :) Restraint often triggers a fear response in these animals. Lifting them off the ground feels life threatening to them. Placing them in a bathtub can be very intimidating and overwhelming to their senses. View the world from their point of view, keep them calm and relaxed, slowly introduce them to new things and sensations, give them time to process and to trust, and they will not feel the need to scream out of fear or stress.

- Bark or "arf": This is a quick, sharp sound they make when they are startled or spooked. It's a very short sound that may be single or repeated several times in quick succession. A very similar sound can be made when the pig or piglet is feeling excited and playful. Cue in on tone and body language to understand if your pig is excited or spooked.

Vocalizations of Demand:

This is not necessarily aggressive or challenging, but it certainly isn't the communication of a well behaved, well-mannered pig-child.

- Screeching
- Screaming
- Hollering

Whichever form it takes, these vocalizations are forceful, LOUD, and long. The pig wants something, and expects to get it. He will gladly use his voice to convey his need. The body language on a demanding pig is confident, tall, head and eyes forward, usually making eye contact, head up. He has something to say and he wants YOU to hear it. His movements are precise and organized; he is in complete control. He may follow you around, pace at the baby gate, or wreak havoc on the house in his frustration. This is VERY different body language and behavior from a scared or fearful pig.

BODY LANGUAGE

Pig behavior & communications can be broken down into three categories:

1. Dominant and/or Challenging
2. Submissive and/or Compliant
3. Fearful, Anxiety and/or Reactive

To understand what a pig is telling you, you first need to understand their perspective of the world. Pigs live in a tight knit social structure within their family. There is a leader that has earned the right to protect the herd. This leader is respected and trusted with the welfare of the herd. If for some reason a pig believes this leader to be lacking, s/he will feel obligated to make a challenge, to overtake the leader. A weak leader is not good for the herd, a weak leader is a vulnerability for the entire family. A weak leader causes stress and strain within the herd. In short - YOU need to be your pig's leader, and you need to be a consistent, strong, worthy leader. If you have earned it, your pig will trust you and respect you. If he has any question of your leadership, he very well may challenge you - not out of spite or hate, but out of concern for the family's safety. Always remember a pig lives the life of a prey animal. At the very core of their existence is self-preservation. While we are happily at the top of the food chain with no predators, and no obvious threats to our life, pigs do not feel that same luxury. When working with your pig, bring lots of compassion and patience. It's not easy being a pig in a human's world!

Dominant, Challenging

There are several reasons for a pig to behave in a dominant or challenging manner. When a stranger comes to the house, the pig may perceive him as a threat or a new herd member, one who needs to be challenged in order to position himself in the correct place of hierarchy, with the strongest and most abled pigs (or humans) being higher up in order to protect the weaker family/herd members from danger and outside threats.

Body Language:

- Tight, stiff, body language
- Confident posture
- Quick, jerky movements
- Moving head first TOWARDS another
- Head swiping (swinging the head to the side in a threatening manner)
- Chomping the jaws or teeth together
- Foaming at the mouth

Submissive and/or Compliant

A submissive pig is a relaxed pig. These pigs acknowledge and respect their place in the family. They understand you are the leader in charge, and they are happy to have someone to protect them. When these pigs are asked to move, they move. They are well trained and follow instruction well. When pigs are comfortable with a leader overseeing their safety, they have loose body language. They happily greet their family when they come home and may even spin around gleefully with the zoomies.

Body Language:

- Relaxed
- Slow moving, care free
- Unobservant
- Ears forward listening, nose up sniffing as they approach for treats
- Casually graze in the yard
- Playful moments of sprinting, galloping, spinning, or zooming around
- Relatively quiet, with happy contented grunts or greetings

Fearful, Anxiety, or Reactive

Pigs that are stressed will show signs of fear and anxiety. These pigs will be very reactive to your movements. If your pig is fearful, it's important to work towards gaining trust and building confidence. Do not punish a pig for fearful behavior. Fearful pigs do not mean to harm, but will lash out if they feel they need to protect themselves. Work carefully with a fearful pig to avoid further damaging trust or provoking aggressive behavior.

Body Language:

- Quick movements
- Loud squealing, squawking, and agitated grunts in protest
- Erratic movements when asked to move
- Body faced towards person
- Eyes focused on person, does not break eye contact

Rooting & Nudging

Rooting is a natural behavior for pigs where the pig uses his snout to push or nudge into something repeatedly. Pigs root in different ways for different reasons: for comfort, to communicate, to cool off, or to search for food. It's important to give your mini pig appropriate outlets for their rooting such as blankets and a patch of yard they can root.

It starts when they are born, piglets root at their mother's teat to trigger milk letdown. This is both instinctual and comforting for piglets. After the piglets are weaned, they will continue to root for comfort similar to toddlers using a pacifier. They will root against their family, blankets, or flooring. Piglets are more likely to root for comfort when they are tired or hungry. Piglets will outgrow this type of rooting as they mature. Piglets that were weaned too early or taken away from their mother will have a harder time outgrowing the need for comfort rooting. To avoid bruises, teach your piglet to root into a blanket or stuffed animal instead of your skin. Simply redirect the piglet to the chosen item when they start rooting. You will need to do this repeatedly until they get the hang of it.

Rooting is used a lot in pig communication at all ages. Pigs will root at your legs gently to politely ask for a bite of food while you're making dinner. They will root hard enough to leave bruises to demand food if they are allowed. They will root your hand to ask for belly rubs if they are feeling neglected. When pigs are intact (not spayed or neutered) they will aggressively root your legs out of sexual frustrations, which usually leads to humping and biting.

When pigs are outdoors they need a way to cool off. If a mud hole or kiddy pool is available, they will use this. If there are no other places to lower their body temperature in the heat, they will use their snout to dig a hole into the cool dirt. If your mini pig is rooting holes to lay in during the summer, consider adding a small pool to prevent overheating.

Pigs are food driven. They naturally use their snout to root in search of food. Outside they will do this by digging up grass or other plants in search of roots and bugs. There is no prevention or training that can stop this. If your pig is becoming destructive in the yard, he will need a fenced area where he is allowed to root.

Rooting is a natural behavior that pigs need an outlet for. Restricting rooting or outdoor time will frustrate the pig causing behavioral issues. When their needs and outdoor time are not met, they may even become obsessive rooters indoors, ruining carpeting or laminate flooring.

Harness and Leash Training

Harness Training by Jessie Brookings of This Little Piggy Mini Pet Pigs in Canada:

Shop for your mini pig harness at www.ThisLittlePetShop.com

Pigs are naturally a flight animal and that is extremely important to remember when you are harness training your piglet. When attempting to harness train your piglet the first step it to purchase a harness that is pig safe. Harnesses that have two buckles (one on the neck and one on the girth) work best. If you have to pick up your piglet to put their feet through a 'step-in' harness you may find it more challenging as your piglet would prefer to keep their feet on the ground.

The second step is to introduce the harness to your piglet in a location in the home that is quiet and the piglet is comfortable in. Place yourself on the floor with some of your piglet's favorite treats (cut up grapes and their pellets work great). Place the harness on the ground in front of you and place some of the treats beside it. Show the piglet where the treats are and allow him to eat them. If the piglet is showing no hesitation with eating beside the harness place treats on top of the harness and allow your piglet to eat them. Once your piglet has demonstrated no hesitation with this step, pick up the harness and hold it STILL in front of the piglet. Offer a treat to the piglet at this time. The goal is to make the harness positive on and off the piglet.

Once the piglet has shown no hesitation to the harness being in the air you may at this time place a few treats on the ground in a pile and while the piglet is having a snack move the harness towards the back of the piglet. Usually at this step you will see them watching your hand and maybe take a step or two to the opposite side of your hand. If they do, hold your hand still until the piglet settles. Do not move the harness back as this motion would encourage the behavior. It is okay to offer more treats if the piglet is still not settled with the harness being at his side.

Once your piglet becomes comfortable with the movement of the harness towards his side continue the movement to placing the harness on his back. There are three important things to remember at this step.

Offer lots of treats are he will step away when the harness touches him. Do not let go of the harness. You want to prevent the harness from falling on the floor and scaring him. Remember you are not trying to fit the harness to the piglet at this time, just placing it on his back.

You may need to work at this step for a few days to get your piglet comfortable with the feeling of the harness on their back.

Once your piglet has become comfortable with all the above steps you can now work with doing up the buckles. This will also be done in small steps and over a period of time if your piglet requires it. Place treats in a pile on the floor and while your piglet is eating place the harness on his back and slowly clip the neck buckle together. Add more treats to the pile and clip the girth buckle. Add more treats to the pile and let your piglet continue to eat his treats while wearing his harness. *It is important for the harness to not be too tight on the piglet through the first couple times you are repeating this last step. You also do not want it so loose the piglet can step their leg through it. You would want it loose but not falling off.

Repeat this step a few times a day while allowing your piglet to wear his harness around the house for a bit at a time. To take the harness off offer some treats in a pile and unclip both buckles. As you can see training your mini pig overall is about reading their body language. It's important to know what it is they are comfortable with and how far you can go with each training session.

Remember, things do not happen overnight. Go slow and allow your piglet to become comfortable with each step before moving along to the next one.

Leash Training:

Once the harness has been mastered, the leash can be introduced. This is a difficult step for some mini pigs as they feel the loss of control over their movements. While introducing the leash, consider the fear and panic a young prey animal must feel when they sense the restraint of a leash. Always use positive reinforcement when training. You want your piglet to enjoy the leash and harness, to understand what is being asked, and to gladly follow your lead. Treats are very helpful in this training, but also use a kind, happy voice and gentle scratches that your piglet enjoys.

Start leash training in a secure area, either indoors or in a safely fenced yard. Do not pull on the leash or expect your mini pig to follow you. Attach the leash and let it drop so the piglet can get used to the weight of it. Once he is comfortable with the weight of the leash, gently pick up the leash. This part goes much easier if you have taught your mini pig to come when called. While holding the leash loosely, call your pig to you. As soon as they take the first step towards you, tell them good pig and offer a reward. Continue to practice this, either by calling them, shaking food in a can, or luring them with delicious treats.

When your piglet is coming when called, without worry of the leash, then it's time to give a little pull. Call your piglet to you, holding the leash. As soon as he turns to take a step towards you, give a very slight pull on the leash. Immediately say good pig and offer a treat. Continue to practice this, giving more and more pressure on the leash as he allows. If he resists the pressure, pulls back, or jumps, then you have pushed too far and you will need to work to regain that trust.

By rewarding your piglet for following the lead of the leash, you will be able to direct him where you want him to go. Never drag or pull a pig on a leash. It is dangerous in that they can wiggle out of their harness, getting loose or hit by a car. This struggle also destroys the trust that you have worked so hard to build up.

Take it slow, be patient, use lots of luring with food and praise for good behavior!

Basic Skills Training

There are a few basic skills to teach your pig so that you may have a well-mannered, easy to control pet. Teaching your pig commands, tricks, and basic skills at a very young age will set him or her up for success. You are teaching them the things that you will need from them to keep them safe and happy and in effect keeping the family proud and in control.

Pigs are highly motivated by food. Teaching tricks and skills are simple with a small, easy to handle and quick to eat reward such as air popped non-salted, non-buttered popcorn, cheerios, shredded wheat, small bite of apple, quartered or halved grape.

Pigs thrive on routine. Training time should be a specific time every day when your pig seems most focused. Not before meal time or when your pig is hungry. Training sessions before bedtime give your pig a great physical and mental workout for a restful night of sleep.

The Command Come

One of the most important of the basic skills is to teach your pig to come. This training starts as easily as speaking the word "Come" every time you offer your pig their meals. Start this day one with your pig and repeat any time a treat is offered or food is given for a couple of days. Start calling for your pig to come from farther and farther distances while rewarding with praise or a healthy treat each time the pig obeys. Fewer and fewer treats and more praise as the days follow and your pig should have this mastered in no time. This command mastered will make harness and leash training much faster and less stressful.

Sit

Teaching your pig to sit may be slightly more challenging, but can also be taught quickly. It's a good skill to build on in future training. You may eventually want your pig to sit quietly to wait for his meals. To teach sit make sure your pig is on carpet or an area rug so that his feet won't slip out from under him.

Get you pig familiar with the treats/reward. Show the pig your reward and lift it in front of their snout and slowly up and over the head. Your pig should raise its snout following the treat. Watch the pig's snout, say "sit" and slowly continue to raise it until the pig's bottom hits the floor. Timing is critical so be sure you reward as soon as that butt hits the floor. Some find it is easier to accomplish a full sit by having their pig close to a wall or in the corner. Some pigs may not respond well if they feel cornered or trapped against a wall. Once the pig's bottom hits the floor say "sit" and praise, praise, praise and reward with the treat.

No

Obviously, the command NO is going to be used often. Pigs learn these short commands easily and fast, so only use NO when it's really needed. Positive reinforcement "good pig" and praise for good behavior can go far in training your pig. You can use other methods of showing your pig incorrect behavior in a number of ways. A loud, firm NO with a stop sign hand or finger pointing will show your pig that you are not pleased with its behavior. Eventually, just raising that stop sign hand or finger may be all you need to get your pigs attention.

Back, Leave It or Out

Back or Leave it can be very helpful for a couple of reasons. If you pig is in an area that he or she shouldn't be or if they are interested in something that they shouldn't be then the Back or Leave it command should cause your pig to do just that, back away or leave it. Teaching this will require a good reading of your pig's body language. When your pig steps into an area, such as the kitchen which may be off limits, you need to say the command and use your body moving toward the pig to make the pig step back. Say "back, back" or "out" with every step and then praise. Start with a couple of steps back from your pig and gradual increase to a few, praising as you go. Soon, just saying the word back should cause steps back from your pig, however you may have to reinforce the training by moving forward a step or two every once in a while.

Wait or Stay

Wait or stay can be a little more challenging to teach because the pig is going to want to scamper to the treat so keep the reward hidden. Have your pig sit and then repeat "stay" with a hand gesture or finger point, which ever hand signal you are not using for "No". After the pig has sat still for a moment or two, praise and reward. Each time waiting longer and longer before rewarding. Gradually, start taking steps back with a reminder of "stay", then return to your pig with praise and reward. Stay can be a little easier to maintain if the pig knows you come to them for reward as opposed to them running to you. This one will take some time, patience and extra practice.

Spin, Dance, Left/Right

This trick can be called a few names. It is basically your pig turning in circles for the reward going to the left or right. You can teach this one easily by using your visible reward overhead moving in a large circle guiding your pig to use his feet to turn. Some say "spin" and some use "left", "right" as they guide the pig to turn both ways. Very easy trick to teach and the pigs seem to enjoy the little dance.

Shake or Wave

Teach your pig to "shake" or "give hoof" by gently touching the back of her hoof, say "shake" and give a treat. After a few times you can use more pressure against the back of the hoof without making her uncomfortable. If you grab the hoof unexpectedly she may panic and back up. Some pigs are more sensitive to this feeling and will need more patience. Others will let you lift their foot without resistance. As soon as the hoof is touched (along the back) or lifted, give your command word and reward. You can mix up rewards between food and verbal rewards. Repeat, repeat, and repeat. Soon your pig will anticipate the hoof lift and will voluntarily lift their foot. Be excited! Reward and tell her what a good girl (or boy) she is! They will feed off your energy and understand the correlation of the command and action. You can either crouch down and put your hand out, or stand and put your foot out. Give the shake command and your pig will set her hoof on your hand/foot. This is shake. To move onto wave you can stand back a little bit, ask for the shake command. With nothing to shake with, your pig will wave her hoof trying to land on something. Tell her "good wave!" as this new trick is born.

Command Words

Word repetition and consistency will teach your pigs many useful skills. Using "bed" or "kennel" every time your pig is put into his or her area repetitively will result in a pig that puts itself to bed at night when told.

The word "potty" can become a command with the use of the word consistently when your pig goes potty.

The word "harness" repeated every time you put the harness on and off can let your pig know that it's time to stand still to get the harness on or off.

Potty Training

Potty training is one of the first things a pig parent will work on with their piglet. This will be a lot easier if you set them up for success from the beginning! First, decide if you want to train your baby to use a litter box or go outside or a combination. Potty training during winter in cold climates limits outside potty training until spring. Consistency in training is essential for success.

Young piglets do not have full bladder control, so many parents choose to start with a litter box until they are old enough to consistently make it outside for potty breaks. Start out with a small area. A puppy pen, a bathroom, a small gated off room, or a baby playpen. Remember, babies need to use the potty often throughout the day. Immediately after waking, after eating, after drinking, after playing and anytime in between.

Training Your Piglet To Potty Outside

Keep them confined to a small, safe area until they get used to the family and environment. Give them a comfortable area to nap with a pet bed or blanket. Take them to the designated outdoor potty area. This area must be safe and secure for your piglet. Never take a piglet out without a harness and leash unless you have a small fenced area or outdoor playpen. Every time they eat, drink, wake from a nap, or has playtime, take them out to potty.

In the beginning you will want to take them to potty many times in a day. If you want your piglet to learn to potty on command, you need to choose command words and use those when you take him/her outside, for example, "go potty" or "go poop," etc. When they do go potty outside tell them "good boy/girl, good potty!!" (in a happy voice). You can even reward them with a treat when they are successful, and they will soon catch on that they have done the right thing. You can either install a doggy door for them to use, or attach a bell to the backdoor and train them to ring it when they need to go out. Remember, accidents are accidents and they are babies.

There is no need to punish; as in dogs, rubbing their nose in their mistake, physical punishment and/or yelling (after the fact) will not help your piglet learn house training skills. If you catch them in the act, you can verbally tell them "no" sternly and quickly show them where they should go.

Training Your Piglet To Potty Inside

It is helpful to ask your breeder what they have been using for litter box training and get the same pellet for familiarity for an easier smooth transition. Breeders most often use horse bedding pellet or pine pellet. Cat litter cannot be used as pigs will eat the kitty litter and it is not good for them.

Keep your piglet confined to a small area when not being held or attended to and keep the litter box in this area. Piglets cannot hold their bladders very long and often do not have time to get to their litter box without an accident.

Do not let your piglet roam the house freely without being attended to, as they will become overwhelmed and forget where the potty box is, be too afraid to go find it, or get distracted. Pigs are clean animals and do not want to soil where they sleep or eat, so keep the litter box in a different corner of their area, away from the bed and food.

Put them in their potty box often and say "go potty". You will want to place your piglet in their litter box every time they eat, drink, and often throughout the day. When your piglet does potty in the appropriate place tell them "good boy/girl!!" in an excited praising voice. You can reward your piglet with a treat in the beginning stages as well. They will soon understand they have done the right thing.

Make sure the sides of your litter box are very low for piglet to enter. If your piglet slips in the litter box or hesitates to enter, cut an entry low enough and line the bottom with paper towels for added traction.

Once they are consistently using the litter box in their small area, increase the amount of space your pig can roam SLOWLY! If they start having accidents, then limit the space again until they are consistently using the box. You may need more then one litter box in the house to accommodate your piglet, especially if you have a larger home or a two story home.

Once you put a litter box down it is best to keep it in the same spot permanently. Once they deem a spot as a potty spot, they will continue to use it as a toilet even if you take away or move the potty box! BEWARE of accidents on carpet.

Once a pig goes to the bathroom on the carpet, it can be extremely difficult ever removing the urine smell, especially if it soaks into the padding. They have an incredible sense of smell and therefore will be called back to that area after many efforts of removing the smell. Making sure your pig has mastered potty training before they freely roam the home is an essential part of potty training successfully.

Potty Troubleshooting

Even the most successfully potty trained pig can have set backs or revert to poor potty behavior. Lapses in potty training may be symptomatic of something else.

If your pig is pottying right outside the box:

Put towels or puppy pads around the perimeter of the potty

box until they get better control. Place them in the potty box often.

If you pig is spraying urine over the side of box:

Get a box with taller sides and cut a walk in entrance for them.

If you pig is pottying in inappropriate places:

If they are going under a bed or under a desk, they're telling you they want privacy. Try a covered litterbox or a plastic tub with a lid with an entry way cut in.

If your piglet is picking spots around the house to potty:

Clean the area thoroughly. Their sense of smell is incredible. Just because we can't smell it, doesn't mean it is gone. Once the odor has been eliminated (tips below) use those spots as "feeding stations." Pigs don't like to potty where they eat. If you sprinkle their pellets and treats over those spots, several times a day, they will view that spot as a place to eat, therefore they'll hesitate to soil the area. If the pig potties where they shouldn't, put a piece of stool or a urine soaked paper towel into the litter box, put pig into the box and tell them "go potty" as they sniff the paper towel.

Are hormones the cause:

Intact pigs are incredibly difficult to potty train because their hormones will drive them to leave their scent to attract a mate. Spayed and neutered pigs are far easier to potty train.

If your pig refuses box:

> If your pig refuses to use the litter box, they might not feel comfortable entering. Make sure there is a short entrance for them. Make sure they feel secure standing in it as pigs do not like slippery surfaces. Experiment with different litter choices. Some pigs have litter preferences and refuse to use litters they don't like.

If you pig was potty trained and now won't use the box.

> A few reasons pigs may stop using their litter box after developing good habits are: a urinary tract infection, soiled litter box not cleaned often enough, other pets (i.e. dogs) have access to the potty area and pig doesn't feel comfortable with potty area/needs more privacy/security, pig has outgrown the litter box and needs a bigger accommodation or pig wants to potty outside, or there are soiled areas in the house that is disrupting their training.

Many pigs naturally prefer to potty outside especially as they mature and develop better control. If your pig does not have a UTI, has a clean box, has the litter they prefer, litter box is big enough and pig still isn't consistently using the box, then try taking them outside to potty several times a day. They may be trying to tell you something...

Litter Choices

Newspaper pellets: These pellets can be found at pet stores in the cat litter section. They are made from compressed recycled paper. One popular brand is Yesterday's News, although store brands are just as effective and lower cost. This litter can be found for ~$12 for 25 pounds.

PROS: The pellets have no odor. This is great for those that don't like the smell of pine. The pellets are tidy. These pellets have excellent absorbing properties, keeping piggy's feet dry. When they become wet, they stay in pellet form and darken, making it easy to scoop out the soiled areas. This litter can be composted and is good for the environment. Safe if ingested in small quantities.

CONS: This litter is more expensive than some other litter options. Some aren't satisfied with the odor control since the pellets have no scent.

Pine pellets: These pellets can be found at pet stores or farm stores such as tractor supply. They will be far more expensive in pet stores, in the cat litter section. The name brand is Feline Pine. These pellets can be found far cheaper at Tractor Supply in the horse bedding section. One brand name is Equine Pine although other brands are widely available. These pellets are about $5-7 for 40 pounds.

PROS: This litter is very cost effective. The pine scent has a pleasant smell for some and covers the urine odor. These pellets have excellent absorbing properties keeping piggy's feet dry. This litter can be composted and is good for the environment. Safe if ingested in small quantities.

CONS: When wet the pellets turn to a sawdust like powder. This powder is more difficult to scoop than whole pellets and is often tracked out of the litter box. Some find the pine and urine odor to smell reminiscent of a barn. It comes in a big heavy bag.

Wood pellets: Pellets sold for wood burning stoves are also used in litter boxes.

Pine shavings: Pine shavings can be found in any pet store, feed store, tractor supply, or Walmart in the small animal section. The prices will vary by location, feed stores are usually the cheapest place to buy, around~$6 for a large bag.

PROS: This litter is cost effective and easy to find. Light weight for hauling around. Safe if ingested in small quantities. This litter can be composted.

CONS: Messy! The lightweight shavings tend to scatter out of the litter box very easily. This is also a tempting material for piglets to root around. They aren't very absorbent, urine can run to the bottom of the litter box and pool up around their hooves causing them to seek an alternative potty spot. Some find the pine and urine odor to smell reminiscent of a barn. The bag is large and bulky for storing.

Puppy pee pads: Puppy Pee Pads can be found at any pet store, Walmart or farm store in the dog section. Prices vary by size and location. They can be found at Amazon.com or eBay.com in large quantities for a better value.

PROS: Lightweight and compact, exceptional for traveling. No messy litter scooping or tracking out of the box. Urine color is obvious and medical concerns can be addressed immediately.

CONS: These pads cannot be composted and are terrible for the environment sitting in landfills. They are one of the more expensive options for a litter box. Some pigs will shred & destroy them. This causes a mess in the house and also ingestion danger. Odor control is minimal. Pads need to be changed after each use. Pads may not contain the amount of urine a pig can hold.

Newspapers: Newspapers can be used but may not be successful. Since the absorbing properties are minimal urine may pool around the pig's feet. This is uncomfortable for pigs and they make seek an alternative potty spot.

PROS: Newspapers are cost effective if you have access to unwanted newspapers. They can be composted and good for the environment.

CONS: Newspapers are not very absorbent. There is no odor control.

Litter-free potty systems: There are several litter free potty systems on the market. These are marketed for dogs and come in various sizes. Some will have fake grass at the top or a plastic grate. You can also create your own with wire grate and pvc pipe.

PROS: Save money in the long run on litter costs. Save the environment- no trees were harmed and landfills won't be used unnecessarily. No messy litter to get tracked in the house or to dispose of. Never run out of litter.

CONS: No odor control. Pan needs to be large enough to contain pig pee flood. Carrying the pan of urine to the toilet for dumping daily can be a balancing act with messy consequences. Brands are:

http://www.porchpotty.com/
https://www.pottypatch.com/
http://www.ebay.com/itm/221556476348
https://www.wizdog.com/

Do Not Use

-Clay cat litter: Clay cat litter is dangerous for pigs. They tend to root around in material and will inhale dust and/or get litter stuck on their snout. Ingestion of this litter can be life threatening through intestinal blockage.

-Corn cob litter: Corn cob litter is an impaction/obstruction hazard for pigs. They may try to eat it even though it is indigestible. If this litter gets stuck in their digestive tract they will need lifesaving surgery.

-Walnut litter: Walnut litter is an impaction/obstruction hazard for pigs. They may try to eat it even though it is indigestible. If this litter gets stuck in their digestive tract they will need lifesaving surgery.

-Cedar shavings or pellets: Cedar does not make a good litter choice because of the toxic aromatic oils. Cedar is toxic causing a variety of health problems in humans and animals that are exposed to it for long periods of time. To use cedar in a litter box puts the cedar right at nose level where the pig must enter and breath multiple times a day.

Litter Pan Ideas

Rubbermaid tub appropriately sized for your pig (the bigger the better!)

Under the bed sweater plastic container

Livestock water tub from farm store, 40 gallon or sized appropriately

Dog crate tray

Rabbit droppings pan

Shallow cat litter box

Covered cat litter box with entrance hole cut

Plastic tote with entrance hole cut (lid on top for privacy)

Kiddy pool

Under washing machine pan

Water heater drip pan

Cement mixing tub or multipurpose tub from Lowes or Home De pot

Urine Clean Up

- An enzyme cleaner such as Nature's Miracle will break down the organic compounds of the urine or feces to eliminate the odor rather than mask it as some cleaners will do. These can be found in the potty training section of any pet store, or in the pet section of Walmart.
- Vinegar and water is also a good cleanser for urine.
- On carpet, spray carpet cleaner over area a little wider than soiled spot. Let soak in for a minute or so. Then sprinkle a generous amount of baking soda over whole wet area. Let sit overnight. The next day the baking soda will have soaked up urine and cleaner. Vacuum up.
- Odormute, it's a powder that you mix with water.

Signs of A UTI

A urinary tract infection may include some, all, or none of these symptoms. Different pigs with a UTI may show different symptoms or overlapping symptoms based on the severity of infection, their overall health, and their tolerance or irritation with the infection. Anytime a UTI is suspected please take a urine sample to the veterinarian's office to be evaluated. This can be obtained from sticking a Tupperware, a pan, or a ladle in the stream while they urinate. If they potty outside it's easiest to catch the urine if you have them on leash so you can be close by when they squat. Urinary tract infections can be brought on by a number of factors: hormonal changes (heat cycle), stress, other infections, strain on the body such as healing from surgery, bladder stones or kidney stones, and sometimes factors that we can't see will play a role. Never assume your pig doesn't have a UTI when something is "off".

Watch for:

-Frequent urination
-Urinating on bedding or urinating while sleeping
-Urinating in several spots during the same potty break
-Straining to urinate
-Fever
-Change in water consumption
-Change in urination frequency, odor, and color
-Decreased appetite
-Lethargy
-Irritability
-In case a urinary tract infection is suspected, veterinary care is required. Take your pig to the vet or catch a urine sample and drop off at the vet's office (store in refrigerator until sample can be

taken to clinic; obtain one as fresh as possible). They can analyze the urine for abnormalities and infection. In case of infection, the veterinarian will prescribe antibiotics.

Traveling & Riding in the Car

Legal Requirements for Travel

While traveling with your mini pig you must be aware that there are USDA guidelines that must be followed when crossing state lines. If you are vacationing with your pets, you will need to contact the USDA for information regarding the state lines you will be crossing. If traveling by air you will need the destination state's requirements to enter as well as the airline's specific requirements.

Shipping requirements vary from state to state. The United States Department of Agriculture (USDA) and Animal and Plant Health Inspection Service (APHIS) are the governing body over these requirements, state by state. You must contact the USDA state vet office for the destination state to get detailed information on that state's requirements for importation of miniature pigs, which are classified as swine, prior to scheduling transport by land or air.

These requirements may include; blood work, vaccinations, permanent identification, USDA health certificate, and entry permit number. There may also be a quarantine requirement. Ask for specifics and get that in writing so you may share it with your vet. Some of the blood work requirements may not be mandatory if your herd has been tested for the year. Ask questions and make notes. The information can vary from person to person, office to office, and state to state.

Please remember that the USDA or APHIS requirements are completely separate and unique to the airline requirements. You must comply with the USDA first, and the airline second for legal shipping into another state.

Ground shipping that crosses state lines will need the same USDA/APHIS requirements be met. A ground transport company may have separate and unique requirements that should be met second to the USDA.

Riding in the Car

Training a pig to ride politely in the car takes patience but can start at any age. The younger the pig is started in training for the car, the easier the transition will be. This is an essential skill for all mini pigs both for fun and emergency situations. Never wait until it's time for vacation or a medical emergency to try to get your pig into the car.

You first need to decide how the pig will get in the car. Do you have a vehicle that the pig can get into easily? Will you lift the pig into the car? Will you use travel stairs or a ramp?

It's also time to decide where your pig will ride. A secure crate is the absolute safest place for your mini pig. Plastic airline crates of adequate size is appropriate. Alternatively, a metal wire crate can also be used. It is advised to use a secondary item to secure the crate door in case of an emergency or crash. A bungee cord can be used across the front of the crate to keep the door from popping open.

Some pig parents prefer to have their pigs ride in their lap, in the seat, or on the floor of the vehicle. NEVER allow a pig to ride unrestrained in the front seat or in your lap when you are driving.

Pigs can be pushy and difficult especially with those bruise inflicting hooves. Do not risk your life or safety. For pigs riding in the seat of a vehicle, their leash can be tied to the headrest to keep them in their designated spot. The same can be done for pigs that are secured in the back of an SUV. Always be aware of the reach your pig has on a leash. Do not tie a pig that can hop over the seatback and hurt themselves hanging by a leash.

When you have prepared for your pig to ride in the vehicle, it is time for desensitization. It is common for pigs to have severe anxiety in the car, causing them to squeal, urinate and/or defecate. If a pig is fearful, have compassion and go at a pace they are comfortable with. Do not throw them in the car and become upset when they poop all over the car!

Place your mini pig's favorite blanket or towel in their designated car riding spot. Gather your mini pig's favorite treat. Place a small pile of this treat (such as diced apples, cut up grapes, pig pellets, or cheerios) in their designated riding spot. At this time, you are not taking your pig for a ride. You are only getting them used to the car. Take them to the car with the engine OFF and the door OPEN, let them get in, or put them in, so their nose lands right in their treat pile. This sets up a positive response to getting in the car. For some pigs the most difficult part is getting them inside the car. Having an immediate and profound reward waiting for them will help them overcome this anxiety.

When they are finished enjoying their treat, let them get out of the vehicle on their own, or help them out if they need help. Do this several times, simply place treats in their designated spot in the car, let them go in and have a snack, then come back out. In, out, in, out, in, out. This will help them to not feel trapped by the vehicle.

Once they are comfortable getting in and out without any

hesitation or anxious body language, you can go for a short drive. To prepare for this drive, ruffle up treats in the folds of their blanket. This will keep them busy and rewarded longer than a simple pile of treats. The food distraction is important as the vehicle starts to drive away. Make this first excursion very short! Drive down to the mailbox or a few houses down the street, turn around and drive back home. All the while be sure to praise your mini pig with a comforting voice. If you are able, also give them petting or scratches to reassure them. Ideally they will have enough treats they will still be distracted when you get back home. Repeat this several times on different days, being sure to not stress out your mini pig. Take these steps as slow as needed, and repeat as many times as necessary for your pig to feel comfortable. Remember, their comfort means no poop!

By now your mini pig is ready for real rides! Take them somewhere fun – to the park, to McDonalds for ice cream, or to the lake to play in the water. The possibilities are endless and your pig will have a rich quality of life with the opportunities their car trips can bring.

Visit the American Mini Pig Store online for Mini Pig Travel & First Aid Kits.

We hope the information provided will get you started off on a road toward a healthy, bonded relationship with your mini pig. Remember patience is key. Support is available We ask that you be an educator in your community. Get out and share the facts about mini pig ownership.

Look for our full version book on all things mini pigs, Mini Pig Care, The AMPA Big Book of Mini Pigs.

Appendix 1

Vegetables

Summer/winter squash
Acorn squash
Amaranth
Arrowroot
Artichoke
Arugula
Asparagus
Banana Squash
Belgian endive
Bamboo shoots
Bell Peppers
Black eyed peas
Black radish
Black Salsify
Bok choy
Burdock root
Butter lettuce
Broccoli
Brussels sprouts
Buttercup squash
Butternut squash
Cabbage/red cabbage
Carrots
Cauliflower
Celery root
Celery
Chayote squash
Cherry tomatoes
Chickweed
Chives
Collard greens
Corn

Cucumbers
Dandelion flowers/leaves
Eggplant
Endive
Fava beans
Fennel
Galangal root
Green beans
Green leaf lettuce
Green soybean/Edamame
Jicama
Kale
Kohlrabi
Leeks
Lettuce
Lima beans
Manoa
Mushrooms
Mustard greens
Okra
Olives
Parsnips
Pea pods
Peanuts unsalted
Peas plantain
Pumpkin
Purple asparagus
Radicchio
Radish and leaves
Red clover
Red leaf lettuce
Rhubarb stem/stalk
(no leaves)
Romaine lettuce

Rutabagas
Shallots
Snow peas
Sorrel
Spinach
Spring baby lettuce
Sugar snap peas
Sweet dumpling squash
Sweet potatoes
Swiss chard
Tomatoes
Turnip greens
Turnips
Wasabi root
Watercress
Winged beans
Winter squash
Yellow squash
Yucca root
Zucchini

Fruits

Apples no seeds
Apricots no pits
Bananas & peel
Bitter melon
Black currants
Blackberries
Blueberries
Boysenberries
Breadfruit
Cactus pear
Cantaloupe
Cape gooseberries
Cherimoya
Cherries no pits
Clementine
Coconut

Cranberries fresh or dried
Dates
Durian
Elderberries blue
Elderberries purple feijoa
Figs
Grapefruit
Grapes
Guava
Honeydew melon
Huckleberries
Jackfruit
Jujube
Kiwi & peels
Kumquats
Lemons
Limes
Loganberries
Lychee
Mango
Mulberries
Nectarine
Pears
Plums no pit
Pomegranate
Pummelo
Quince
Raspberries
Red banana
Red currants
Sapodillas
Sharon fruit
Starfruit
Strawberries
Tangerines
Thimbleberry
Watermelon & rind

Grains

Amaranth
Barley
Buckwheat
Brown rice cooked
Corn
Farro
Freekah
Millet
Oats/Oatmeal
Quinoa
Rye
Sorghum/Milo
Teff
Wheat varieties:
Spelt
Emmer
Faro
Einkorn
Durum
Bulgur
Cracked wheat
Wheat berries

Nuts & Seeds Unsalted

Almonds
Cashews
Chia seeds
Cumin seeds
Brazil nuts
Black oil Sunflower seeds
Flax seeds in moderation
Grape seeds
Hazelnuts
Hemp hearts & seeds
Macadamia nuts
Papaya seeds
Peanuts

Pecans
Pine nuts
Pistachios
Pomegranate seeds
Pumpkin seeds
Sunflower seeds
Walnuts
Wheat germ

Legumes-Cooked/No canned

Alfalfa
Black beans
Black eyed peas
Boston beans
Chick peas
Fava beans
Field peas
Kidney beans
Lentils
Lima beans
Mayocoba beans
Mung beans
Navy beans
Pinto beans
Red beans
Split peas

Toxic Food & Plants

Salt
Green/unripe acorns
Young oak leaves
Moldy walnut shells
Elderberries, red
Lima beans raw
Kidney beans raw
Decayed sweet potatoes
Castor beans

Tomato leaves & vine
Avacado skin & pit
Corn stalks
Rhubarb leaves
Potato leaves & green part
Apple leaves & seeds
Apricot leaves & seeds
Pear leaves & seeds
Peach leaves & seeds
Nectarine leaves & seeds
Cherry leaves & seeds
Plum leaves & seeds
Broccoli roots & seeds
Cabbage roots & seeds
Mustard roots & seeds
Tobacco leaves
Nutmeg in large quantities
Lychee seeds
Rambutan raw seeds
Longan seeds
Taro raw
Cassava roots & leaves
Almond leaves

Plants that may cause Photo Sensitivity

Bishop's weed
Parsnip tops
Parsley
Celery tops
Giant hog weed
Buckwheat
Saint John's Wort

HOW CAN YOU HELP IN THE MINI PIG COMMUNITY

BE AN AMPA AMBASSADOR

Get out into the community with your mini pig and educate on the facts of pig ownership. Join mini pig Facebook groups and support your fellow and future mini pig owners. Refer those interested in adding a mini pig to the family to the American Mini Pig Association website and the AMPA breeder map.

DONATE TO HELP EDUCATE

Donate to American Mini Pig Education, 501c3 nonprofit via paypal at education@americanminipigassociation.com

VOLUNTEER:

Rescues and sanctuaries depend on volunteers to accomplish the many tasks involved with caring for the animals. You can volunteer your time, your efforts, and your skills or talents. Contact your local sanctuary to get a list of duties they need accomplished. Contact sanctuaries across the United States to offer assistance with duties that can be done remotely.

DROP OFF DONATIONS:

These can be donations that you purchase in order to donate or you can ask stores to donate for the rescue. A great idea is to can have a "donation collection party". Ask all your friends over for a bar-b-q or wine night asking them to only bring supplies for the local sanctuary or rescue. A blanket donation party or a pig feed party would be fun and make a huge difference to those in need. Get the kids involved! Kids can make a huge impact in collecting donations while teaching them of kindness and generosity to those in need.

FOSTER:

Fostering a pig is not a good fit for everyone. However, if you are willing and able, you can literally save a life by fostering until the animal is vetted, healthy, and finds an appropriate adoptive home. Before accepting a foster animal you must understand where the responsibilities lie. Each organization will have different expectations of the foster family. Typically the foster family will provide food and housing while the rescue will provide or pay for medical care and emergencies. You'll want to get the details in writing before accepting the animal into your home.

Use AMPA Mini Pig Classifieds to connect with other pig people.

ADOPT:

Adopting is a huge decision and should not be made lightly. If you are looking to add a pig to your family, there is a huge selection of rescue pigs of all shapes, sizes, ages, and personalities. Finding the right match is absolutely crucial. Start by making contact with your local sanctuary or rescue to ensure a rescue pig is what you are looking for. They may have one available for adoption or lead you in the direction of one.

Use AMPA Mini Pig Classifieds to connect with other pig people.

TRANSPORT:

Rescuing pigs may require transportation. Drivers are always needed and appreciated. You may offer assistance to drive a pig to the veterinarian for a checkup or procedure, pick them up from the shelter or previous home to drop them off at the rescue/sanctuary/foster home, drive a short leg of a long distance travel, or drive a long distance trip. Always use precautions to ensure the safety of the pig and driver while traveling. If the pig will cross state lines you will need to plan ahead to ensure all state and federal laws are followed.

Use AMPA Mini Pig Classifieds to connect with other pig people.

NETWORK:

Networking can be done from anywhere while saving countless lives! You can network adoptable animals, animals needing rescued, needs of the rescue (donations, fundraisers, transport). Networking can be done through email, Facebook, twitter, media, friends, or any way to get exposure for the rescue organization.

Use AMPA Mini Pig Classifieds to connect with other pig people.

SPONSOR A PIG:

Sanctuaries take on the care of animals that have been abused, abandoned, or neglected. This long term commitment plays a vital role in the pig community as there are FAR MORE pigs in need than homes willing/able to accommodate them. Unfortunately, this leaves a huge ongoing financial burden on the organizations and many have been crushed under the weight of this responsibility. By choosing one animal to "sponsor" you can setup recurring monthly payments of a small amount such as $25 or $50 per month. This will take the burden off the rescue for the basic costs of that animal and allows their resources to be used for more urgent matters such as medical bills and barn maintenance.

American Mini Pig Rescue Sponsorship Program at www.americanminipigrescue.com

Use AMPA Mini Pig Classifieds to connect with other pig people.

SHOP AMAZON SMILE:

http://smile.amazon.com/

Do your shopping on Amazon with a % of the sales going to help a rescue or sanctuary in need. You have to access amazon through the Amazon Smile link and select the organization you would like to benefit from the donated portion of your purchases.

SHOP iGive:

iGive.com

From the iGive website:

Shop at any of the 1,400+ online stores. It's fast and automatic with the iGive button, our Android/iPad apps, or simply use our site to visit stores. You never pay more. We always show you how much you're raising before you buy.
Just about anything you buy counts. We take care of the details, including sending the money you've helped raise to your cause. Donations range from 0.5% to over 20%, varying by store. A typical shopper raises over $100/yr.

AMAZON WISH LIST:

Shop for the pigs in a sanctuary or rescue. An organization can list items needed on their wish list. You purchase the items of your choice to be shipped directly to the sanctuary/rescue.

Shop the American Mini Pig Rescue Amazon Wishlist

SUPPORT SPAY/NEUTER ASSISTANCE PROGRAMS:

Seek out spay and neuter assistance programs. You can help by donating financially, sponsoring a spay or neuter, or spreading the word of such a worthwhile cause to get more donors and pig parents in need involved. You can donate for spay/neuters via paypal to rescueadvocates@americanminipigrescue.com

GAS CARDS:

Rescues tend to put a lot of miles on their cars, and their cars typically have to be on the larger size to accommodate crates and animals.

DIRECT DONATIONS:

Contribute financially to a rescue or sanctuary. This can usually be done from their website or through www.paypal.com. These donations are crucial for nonprofits to operate and care for the animals in their care.

Donate to American Mini Pig Rescue via paypal at rescueadvocates@americanminipigrescue.com

SUPPORT FUNDRAISERS:

Rescues and sanctuaries typically have fundraisers to help with the costs of caring for the animals in their care. You can support these fundraisers by: organizing a fundraiser, donating items to the fundraiser, buying or bidding on items in the fundraiser. If you own a business you can also offer a percentage of sales to be donated to a rescue or sanctuary. This is a double bonus because you are getting exposure for your business/products while also getting exposure for the rescue and their needs. If you are a representative of a company such as Origami Owl or nail wraps, host a party with proceeds donated to a sanctuary or rescue.